THE RACE QUESTION IN MODERN SCIENCE

RACIAL MYTHS

by
JUAN COMAS

*Professor of Anthropology
at the Mexican School of Anthropology*

GREENWOOD PRESS, PUBLISHERS
WESTPORT, CONNECTICUT

Library of Congress Cataloging in Publication Data

Comas, Juan, 1900-
    Racial myths.

    Translation of Los mitos raciales.
    Reprint of the 1965 ed. published by UNESCO, Paris in
its series: The Race question in modern science and
issued as UNESCO publication 891.
    Bibliography: p.
    1. Race. I. Title. II. Series: United Nations
Educational, Scientific and Cultural Organization. The
race question in modern science. III. Series: United
Nations Educational, Scientific and Cultural Organization. UNESCO publication ; 891.
GN269.C6513 1976   572   76-5909
ISBN 0-8371-8801-6

572
C 728

Originally published in 1951 by UNESCO, Paris

This is an authorized facsimile of the original book as first
published in 1951 by Unesco and was produced by arrangement
with Unesco.

Reprinted in 1976 by Greenwood Press,
a division of Williamhouse-Regency Inc.

Library of Congress Catalog Card Number 76-5909

ISBN 0-8371-8801-6

Printed in the United States of America

CONTENTS

The opinions expressed in this volume
are those of the authors and do not necessarily reflect
the views of Unesco.

GENERAL OBSERVATIONS ON RACIAL PREJUDICES AND MYTHS[1]

It is a matter of observation that men are not alike in appearance; there are variations in the external physical characteristics transmitted wholly or partially from father to son. It is groups relatively homogeneous in this respect which constitute what are commonly called 'races'. Not only do such races differ in appearance; they are also usually at different levels of development, some of them enjoying all the blessings of an advanced civilization while others are backward to a greater or lesser extent. This last fact is the true *fons et origo* of racism in all its subsequent developments.

In the Old Testament we already find the belief that the physical and mental differences between individuals and groups alike are congenital, hereditary and unchangeable. The Book of Genesis contains passages apparently assuming the inferiority of certain groups to others: 'Cursed be Canaan; a servant of servants shall he be unto his brethren', while

---

1. For examples of race prejudice extensive use has been made of Sir Alan Burns' excellent little book, *Colour Prejudice* (London, 1948, George Allen and Unwin Limited) which also includes many valuable quotations from works or reviews not available to the present writer. As the nature of the present collection precludes frequent footnotes, the author takes this opportunity to acknowledge his debt to Sir Alan Burns and to express his gratitude for permission to draw on Sir Alan's knowledge.

some sort of biological superiority is implied in the assertion that Jehovah made a compact with Abraham and 'his seed'.

In the New Testament on the other hand, the theme of the universal brotherhood of men is quite incompatible with this point of view.

It is a fact that the majority of religions disregard individual physical differences and regard all men as brothers and equal in the sight of God.

Christianity—though not all Christians—has been anti-racist from the very beginning. St. Paul says: 'There is neither Jew nor Greek, there is neither bond nor free for ye are all one in Christ Jesus', and again: 'He hath made of one blood all nations of men for to dwell on the face of the earth'. We may also recall that traditionally one of the three Magi was a Negro. Racism was condemned by Pope Pius XI and in 1938 the Vatican condemned racist movements as 'apostacy from the Christian faith in spirit and in doctrine'. Moreover the Church's role of the Beatified and of the Saints includes white men, yellow men and Negroes. The 12 apostles themselves were Semitic and so was Mary, mother of Jesus Christ.

Similarly, Mohammedans have never displayed racial intransigence or intolerance to other peoples so long as those peoples adopted the Faith.

Against all this, however, it must be pointed out that we have examples of a contrary attitude from the remotest antiquity. The most ancient reference to discrimination against Negroes, though possibly dictated by political reasons rather than by race prejudice, is found in a stele raised by order of the Pharaoh Sesostris III (1887-49 B.C.) above the second cataract on the Nile:

'Southern Boundary. Raised in the eighth year of the reign of Sesostris III, King of Upper and Lower Egypt, to whom be life throughout all ages. No Negro shall cross this boundary by water of by land, by ship or with his flocks save for the purpose of trade or to make purchases in some post. Negroes so crossing shall be treated with hospitality but no Negroes shall hereafter forever proceed by ship below the point of Heh.'

The Greeks of 2,000 years ago regarded all men not of their own race as 'barbarians', and Herodotus tells us that the Persians in their turn thought themselves greatly superior to the rest of humanity.

To justify the Greek ambition for universal hegemony, Aristotle (384-22 B.C.) evolved the hypothesis that certain

8

peoples are by nature free from birth and others slaves (a hypothesis used, as we shall see, in the sixteenth century to justify the enslavement of Negroes and Amerindians). Cicero however thought otherwise: 'Men differ in knowledge but all are equal in ability to learn; there is no race which, guided by reason, cannot obtain virtue.'

Ideas as to the 'superiority' or 'inferiority' of a people or group of people are subject to constant revision. For proof of this it is enough to recall Cicero's opinion of the Celts of Britain, whom he inconsistently describes, in a letter to Atticus, as exceptionally 'stupid and unteachable'.

The savagery and mystery of Africa which was slowly yielding its secrets to Europeans at the end of the nineteenth century are brought out strikingly in Conrad's great tale *Heart of Darkness,* which draws a parallel with the impression made by the untamed Thames of 1,900 years ago on the captain of a Mediterranean trireme or on the young patrician newcomer from Rome; the latter felt the same 'longing to escape, the powerless disgust, the surrender, the hate', as the colonial administrator of our own day. It is almost redundant to recall the contempt of the Norman nobility for the conquered Saxons, and how the ancestors of the proudest nation of Europe were despised. These are not however, strictly speaking, examples of 'racism', nor had even the fierce antagonism of Christians to Musulmans a racial basis. Hatred or aversion springing from differences in cultural level or religious belief is more human than prejudice claiming to be based on implacable laws of heredity.

All this notwithstanding, it may be asserted that generally speaking there was no true racial prejudice before the fifteenth century, since before then the division of mankind was not so much into antagonistic races as into 'Christians and infidels'—a much more humane differentiation, since the chasm between religions can be bridged while the biological racial barrier is impassable.

With the beginning of African colonization and the discovery of America and of the trans-Pacific sea route to India, there was a considerable increase in race and colour prejudice. It can be explained on grounds of economic self-interest, the resurgence of the imperialistic colonizing spirit, etc. Juan Ginés de Sepulveda (1550) in an attempt to justify the institution of slavery on the strength of the Aristotelian hypothesis, spoke of the inferiority and natural perversity of the American Aborigines, asserted that they were 'irrational beings', that

9

'Indians are as different from Spaniards as cruelty is from kindness and as monkeys are from men'.

Of course there was Fray Bartolemé de Las Casas to maintain the opposite view and battle unwearyingly for the proposition that all the peoples of the world are men and not 'submen' or 'half-men' predestined to do what others tell them. The main basis for social stratification in Latin America was racial discrimination, the order of excellence being Creoles, half-breeds, Indians and Negroes. In theory the law does not recognize such discrimination, but now, as then, the law is not obeyed.

Speaking of the Brazilian Indian, Montaigne (1533-92) said: 'There is nothing savage or barbarous about this nation save for the fact that each of us labels whatever is not among the customs of his own peoples as barbarism'; he was followed in this view by some of the most illustrious thinkers of the eighteenth and nineteenth centuries. Voltaire (1694-1778). J. J. Rousseau (1712-78) and Buffon (1706-88) were among many determined supporters of the fundamental oneness of human nature and hence of the equality of all men. In the other camp Hume (1711-76) wrote: 'I am inclined to believe that Negroes are naturally inferior to whites'. Renan (1823-92) was another who refused to accept the hypothesis of the equality of men and Taine (1828-93) also combated the theory and denied that 'Greeks, barbarians, Hindus, the man of the Renaissance and the man of the eighteenth century are all cast in the same mould'.

Despite the influence of certain thinkers, race prejudice developed into a regular doctrinal system during the eighteenth and nineteenth centuries. There was indeed a relatively brief period when it appeared as though the spread of the principles of the French and American revolutions and the success of the anti-slavery campaign in England might lessen or even abolish such prejudice, but both the reaction which followed the Restoration and the industrial revolution in Europe at the beginning of the last century had direct and damaging repercussions on the racial question. The development of power spinning and weaving opened ever wider markets to cotton manufacturers, and 'Cotton was king', particularly in the Southern part of the United States. The result was an increasing demand for servile labour; slavery, which was breaking down in America and might have vanished of itself, automatically became a sacrosanct institution on which the prosperity of the Cotton Belt depended. It was to defend this so-called 'special institution' that Southern thinkers and sociologists developed a complete pseudo-scientific mythology designed to justify a state of affairs clean contrary to the democratic beliefs they professed. For the quietening of consciences men had to be persuaded that the Black was not merely an inferior being to the White but little different from the brutes.

The Darwinian theory of the survival of the fittest was warmly welcomed by the whites as an argument supporting and confirming their policy of expansion and aggression at the expense of the 'inferior' peoples. As Darwin's theory was made public in the years in which the greater powers were building their colonial empires, it helped to justify them in their own eyes and before the rest of mankind: That slavery or death brought to 'inferior' human groups by European rifles and machine-guns was no more than the implementation of the theory of the replacement of an inferior by a superior human society. In international politics racism excuses aggression, for the aggressor no longer feels himself bound by any consideration for foreigners belonging to 'inferior' races and classifiable little, if at all, above the beasts.

The notion that the stronger is biologically and scientifically justified in destroying the weaker has been applied as much to conflicts within as to those between nations.

It is unfair to level at Darwin—as many have done—the reproach that he promoted this hateful and inhuman theory: the truth is that with coloured societies becoming potential competitors in the labour market and claiming the social advantages regarded as exclusively the heritage of the whites, the latter were obviously in need of some disguise for the utter economic materialism which led them to deny the 'inferior' peoples any share in the privileges they themselves enjoyed. For that reason they welcomed with satisfaction Darwin's biological thesis and then by simplification, distortion and adaptation of it in conformity with their own particular interests, transformed it into the so-called 'social Darwinism' on which they based their right to their social and economic privileges; it is a thing which bears no relationship to Darwin's purely biological principles. Herbert Spencer (1820-1903) applied to sociology the concept of 'survival of the fittest' and the same idea was used to defend Nietzsche's (1844-1900) doctrine of the 'superman' with whom 'fittest' was equated.

In this way progress in biology was misused to provide

11

superficially scientific and simple solutions to allay scruples on points of human conduct. However, the distance between science and myth is both brief and easily traversed and that is what happened in this case.

It is obvious that the psycho-somatic inheritance does influence the external appearance and the conduct of human beings, but that does not warrant the argument of the racists that (a) biological heredity is the sole important factor or (b) that group heredity is as much a fact as individual heredity.

Racist doctrine becomes more dangerous still when it is applied, not to separate ethnic groups, but to different social classes within the *same group*. For instance, Erich Suchsland (*Archiv für Rassen und Gesellschafts-Biologie*), argues the thesis that the individuals unsuccessful in life (for instance, those who lack the means to live in the more expensive suburbs) are necessarily the racially inferior elements in the population, whereas the rich are 'racially superior'; hence the bombardment of poor quarters would be a form of selection and would bring racial improvement. Here there is no question of white against black or nordic against non-Aryan; it is a question of finding pseudo-biological support for discrimination against the proletarian classes by the bourgeoisie. Even without any explicit admission, it is quite obvious that racial or class discrimination in this and other instances hides a social-economic antagonism. Alexis Carrel (*Man the Unknown*) does not go as far as Suchsland, but nevertheless maintains that the proletariat and the unemployed are people who are inferior by heredity and descent—men inherently lacking the strength to fight, who have sunk to the level at which fighting is no longer necessary: as though the proletariat did not have a far sterner fight every hour of the day than the well-to-do.

Prenant suggests as a possibility that the main concern of many racists may be, not to provide an apparently objective basis for nationalism and patriotism, but to inculcate the notion that social phenomena are governed by racial factors determined once and for all. Such a biological determinism, unalterable by social action, would absolve Society of all responsibility for each man's heredity, would determine at birth whether he was going to be a great man, a capitalist, a technician, a member of the proletariat or even one of the unemployed, without anyone being able to do anything effective to prevent it.

In any case there is no room for doubt that 'racial' discrimination is only one facet of the broader problem of social discrimination.

The notion of 'race' is so charged with emotional force that objective discussion of its significance in relation to social problems is uncommonly difficult. *There is no scientific basis whatsoever* for a general classification of races according to a scale of relative superiority, and racial prejudices and myths are no more than a means of finding a scapegoat when the position of individuals and the cohesion of a group are threatened.

Persons differing in physical appearance are easily identifiable targets for aggression, while in psychological terms the feeling of 'guilt' is removed or mitigated, given a more or less plausible 'scientific' theory whereby it can be shown that the group attacked is 'inferior' or 'harmful'. Generally speaking, such 'aggression' is directed either against minority groups or against cowed and powerless majority groups.

This brief outline of the origin, development and alleged justification for racial prejudices and myths in general will serve as an introduction for the more detailed analysis of certain of the more widespread and fundamental myths of the racist theory. We hope to demonstrate the falsity and error of these pseudo-biological arguments which are no more than a smoke-screen for their proponents' oppressive aims and policies.

THE MYTH OF BLOOD AND OF THE INFERIORITY OF CROSS-BREEDS

Human miscegenation has been and is the subject of infinite debate. Opinions on the subject are conditioned by the views of the disputants on race and racial differences, the opponents of miscegenation starting from the assumption of racial inequality, whereas its defenders take the view that the differences between human groups are not such as to constitute an objection to cross-breeding between them. Hence the first thing needed in the study of the problems raised by human inter-breeding is a clear definition of what is meant by race and the selection of criteria for deciding whether or not any pure races exist.

Even under the loosest definition, race implies the existence of groups presenting certain similarities in somatic characteristics which are perpetuated according to the laws of biological inheritance, allowing for a margin of individual variation.

The peoples of Europe are of such mongrel origin that any attempt at classification according to only two characteristics (colour of eyes and hair) would exclude two-thirds of the population in any region studied; the addition of a third characteristic (cranial formation) would leave us with a still smaller fraction of the population presenting the required combination of all three characteristics; and with the inclusion of stature and nasal index, the proportion of 'pure' types would become infinitesimal.

We may take it then that there are no pure human races; at the very most it would be possible to define a pure race in terms of the incidence of one selected somatic characteristic, but never in terms of all or even of the majority of hereditary traits. Nevertheless there is a widespread belief that there was a time in antiquity when racial types were pure, that miscegenation is of relatively recent date, and that it threatens humanity with a general degeneration and retrogression. This belief lacks the slightest support from science. The mixing of races has been going on since the very beginning of human life on earth, though obviously the improvement of communications and the general increase in population has stimulated it in the last two centuries. Migration is as old as the human race, and automatically implies cross-breeding between groups. It is quite possible that the Cro-Magnon type of the upper Paleolithic interbred with Neanderthal man, as seems to be indicated by the discovery of remains displaying intermediate characteristics. Moreover the existence of Negroid and Mongoloid races in prehistoric Europe is a further proof that cross-breeding is not a recent phenomenon, and that the oldest populations of Europe are no more than the product of such miscegenation over thousands of years. Yet they show neither the disharmony nor the degeneration which many writers believe to result from racial interbreeding.

History shows us that all the areas in which a high culture has developed have been the scene of the conquest of an indigenous race by foreign nomadic groups, followed by the breaking down of caste divisions and the creation of new amalgams; these, though regarded as racially homogeneous nations, were in fact no more than new nationalities comprising different races.

Those who, like Jon A. Mjoen consider miscegenation

dangerous for the future of mankind, assert that it is a source of physical degeneracy and that immunity against certain diseases diminishes. They allege that prostitutes and vagrants are commoner among half-bred than among pure-bred races, while an increased incidence of tuberculosis and other diseases is observable among the former group, with a diminution of mental balance or vigour and, an increase in criminal tendencies (*Harmonic and Disharmonic Race Crossing and Harmonic and Unharmonic Crossings, 1922*). These data are not valid because the writer does not specify the types of individuals studied nor the general characteristics of the races which have interbred; he ought also to prove that the specific families whose interbreeding produced the half-breeds examined were physically and mentally healthy and free of any sign of degeneracy or disability. Mjoen also entirely overlooks the influence of the social background on the subjects' behaviour.

C. B. Davenport also demonstrates (in *The Effects of Racial Miscegenation, 1917*) the existence of disharmonic phenomena in half-breeds—relatively small digestive organs in a bulky body, well developed teeth in weak jaws, large thighs out of proportion to the body, etc. It is not disputed that there are individuals displaying such characteristics, but it has not been shown that the phenomena are due to miscegenation; similar cases are found among old families while generally speaking crossbreeding between black and white produces well proportioned individuals.

S. K. Humphrey, M. Grant, L. Stoddard and many others argue that, as a result of crossbreeding with foreign elements, there is a likelihood of the North American population losing its present stable and harmonic character. Some writers have gone so far as to assert that such a disharmony would be productive of a whole series of social evils and immoral tendencies.

A line of reasoning rebutting the validity of such arguments as those under discussion is that advanced by H. Lundeborg (*Hybrid-types of the Human Race, 1931*), demonstrating that miscegenation is more frequent among the lower social classes than among the middle and upper classes: hence the phenomena observed by Mjoen and Davenport are due not to the assumed correlation between hybridism and degeneracy or debility, but to the fact that it takes place between individuals belonging to the most impoverished sections of the human groups concerned. The same phenomena would result from endogamy as from exogamy and the interbreeding of races

15

has nothing to do with it. In point of fact the human families in which endogamy has been consistently practiced are frequently marked by a degree of degeneracy equal to or even greater than that which Mjoen and Davenport purport to find in half-breeds.

Both endogamy and exogamy are utilized according to the requirements of the case for the improvement of animal strains; if a strain is good from the point of view of the characteristics interesting the stock-breeder, inbreeding can be continued for many generations without outside crosses and without exhibiting signs of degeneracy. Endogamy further serves to reveal all the hereditary potentialities of a group as it brings out all the recessive hereditary characteristics which would remain latent if they existed in one of the parents only; in such cases, if the characteristic in question is undesirable, the logical and necessary step is exogamic crossing (miscegenation) so as to introduce a dominant hereditary factor to counter the undesirable recessive characteristic.

Thus the immediate result of crossbreeding is to check the outward manifestation of any recessive defects peculiar to either of the races interbreeding. In other words, endogamy makes recessive anomalies and defects visible or tangible, whereas exogamy tends to extirpate or, at the least, to minimize them.

The same line of reasoning can be applied in the case of useful hereditary talents, characteristics and aptitudes. Hence, it is impossible to assert in general terms that the effects of endogamy or exogamy on the descendants of such unions are good or bad; the nature of the result depends in each case on the genetic characteristics of the individual's interbreeding.

The champions of miscegenation argue that endogamy or marriage between members of the same group conduces to the deterioration of the race, and that hybrid races are more vigorous because the infusion of 'new blood' increases the vitality of the group, etc. This dangerous generalization can be refuted by the same arguments as the first.

Neither the partisans nor the enemies of miscegenation have determined certain aspects of the question, which the writer feels should be examined: (a) results of miscegenation between groups definitely above the average and more particularly between groups definitely below the average; (b) the form taken by the environmental obstacles against which half-breeds usually have to fight.

If half-breeds in any country are treated by law or custom

as second-class citizens (from the social, economic and political point of view), it is highly probable that their cultural contributions will not be commensurate with their innate abilities. Under a rigid caste system in which there is no possibility of a half-breed's raising himself above the social status of the lower-caste parent, clearly any assessment of the effects of racial miscegenation should not be based on the level attained by individuals of mixed blood. On the other hand, under a system where individual merit alone is the basis for social classification, the achievements of half-breeds would be a very definite indication of their intrinsic qualities.

It is, in fact, difficult to distinguish between the effects of racial miscegenation as such and those of crossbreeding between lower-grade population groups independently of their race. Instances of interbreeding between groups higher in the social scale have produced a large proportion of high-grade human beings, but in none of these cases should the results be attributed exclusively to the cross. In the present state of our knowledge there is nothing to prove that crossbreeding produces either degeneracy in the descendants of the cross or groups of improved quality.

The notion of humanity as being divided into completely separate racial compartments is inaccurate. It is based on false premises, and more particularly on the 'blood' theory of heredity which is as false as the old racist theory. 'Of one blood' is a phrase without meaning, since the genes or factors of heredity have no connexion whatever with the blood, and are independent elements which not only do not amalgamate but tend to become most sharply differentiated. Heredity is not a fluid transmitted through the blood, nor is it true that the different 'bloods' of the progenitors are mixed and combined in their offspring.

The myth of 'blood' as the decisive criterion regarding the value of a cross persists even in our own day and men still speak of 'blood' as the vehicle of inherited qualities, 'of my own blood', 'the voice of blood', 'mixed blood', 'new blood', 'half blood', etc. The terms, 'blue blood' and 'plebeian blood' have become a permanent part of everyday speech as descriptions of the descendants of aristocratic and plebeian families respectively, the last being used in a depreciative sense. 'Blood' is also the mean nationality: 'German blood', 'Spanish blood', 'Jewish blood', etc. The criterion reaches the nadir of absurdity in such cases as the classification in the United States of those individuals as 'Negroes' or 'Indians' who have one-sixteenth part of 'Indian blood' or 'black blood'—that is, when one of their sixteen direct ancestors (great-great-grand-parents) was a Negro or an Indian.

People who still think in this way are quite incapable of understanding the inwardness of hereditary phenomena or of the social phenomena in which heredity plays a part. If there is inheritance by blood how are we to explain why children of the same parents differ in character when the *same blood* runs in their veins? Again, how are we to explain why certain individuals exhibit characteristics found in their grandparents but absent in their parents?

The truth is that many people are ignorant of the fact not only that the blood has nothing whatever to do with the genetic process, but that it has also been proved that the mother does not supply blood to the foetus which develops its own blood from the beginning (F. M. Ashley-Montagu, *The Myth of Blood,* 1943)—this indeed explains why a child may be of a different blood group from its mother.

Lastly, the fact that successful blood transfusion between individuals of different races is possible, given congruity of serological types, is a new and striking proof that the 'myth of blood' lacks the slightest biological foundation.

It is beyond dispute that all the major races are of hybrid origin, and during the millenia which have elapsed since the original fission of the basic human stock, crossings have gone on continuously. Dixon points out that the brachycephalic Alpines despised by Grant and others were an important element in the building of the Babylonian culture; that the immigration of the Alpine Dorians into Greece immediately preceded the flowering of Hellenic culture; that Rome did not attain its full glory until after the conquest by an Alpine stock of the Mediterranean-Caspian population of Latium; that the development of Chinese culture followed the absorption of Caspian by Alpine elements; and that the amazing development of modern European civilization has occurred in the zone where the mixture of Alpines, Mediterraneans and Caspians has gone farther than anywhere else in the world. There are many other examples of great civilizations such as Egypt, Mesopotamia and India arising at the points where different peoples mingled.

Of course racists such as Gobineau, who regard miscegenation as necessarily disastrous, are capable of such absurdities as to claim that of the 10 most brilliant known civilizations, six are the work of 'Aryans', the 'higher' branch of the

18

white race (Hindu, Egyptian, Assyrian, Greek, Roman and German); while the other four major civilizations (Chinese, Mexican, Peruvian and Maya) are the work of the white race slightly interbred with inferior races. Gobineau concludes that the signs of degeneracy occurring in cross-bred stock are egalitarian ideas, democratic movements, etc., and that miscegenation, produces mediocrities, as it were 'men with the herd mind', 'nations dulled by a fatal somnolence' . . . 'people like buffaloes chewing the cud in the stagnant wallows of the Pontine marshes'. It is unnecessary to refute yet again ideas so absurd, based solely on racist criteria of a political and philosophical nature and on pseudo-scientific biological arguments which have already been discussed and rebutted.

By way of examples of crossbreeding in what are accepted as civilized nations, from the earliest ages England (Britain) was occupied by human groups of the Cro-Magnon type and by Nordics, Mediterraneans and Alpines, and in later ages was invaded by Saxons, Norwegians, Danes and Normans. Thus far from it being possible in our day to speak of a pure English race, we have an excellent example there of a racial mosaic.

In the Palaeolithic Age France was settled by a number of different races, Neanderthal, Cro-Magnon, Chancelade and Grimaldi; in the Neolithic Age a number of branches of the Mediterranean race and certain primitive Alpines came in from the east and in the seventh century B.C. Celtic invaders conquered the first colonists. About the first century of our own era France had a foretaste of the barbarian invasion which was, however, contained for the time being by the power of Rome; two centuries later the Vandals conquered Gaul and the Visigoths founded a kingdom in southern France which continued in existence until the eighth century. Even these few points give an idea of the degree of racial heterogeneity in France and show the extent of the interbreeding which has taken place. 'Western France is perhaps more Teutonic than south-western Germany and much of eastern Germany is more Slavonic than Russia.'

The course of events has been very similar in other continents, and if we get the impression that the mixture of races has been carried to its farthest point in post-Columbian America this is merely because the phenomenon of interbreeding is occurring before our eyes and is not merely a record in the history books. It should further be recalled that the pre-Columbian population of America was also heterogeneous in nature from the beginning.

In all the regions in which an advanced culture is found there has been conquest of one people or peoples by others. The claim that crossbreeds are degenerate is refuted by the actual fact that the whole population of the world is hybrid and becoming increasingly so. Isolated human groups have had little or no influence on the cultural progress of humanity, whereas the conditions which allow of any group playing an important role in civilization are promoted by crossing with other races.

The influence of Caspian-Mediterranean immigrants into Northern Italy may well have been a factor in the brilliance of the Renaissance in that area. Again, is it mere coincidence that a European culture, after the Dark Ages, began to emerge at the point in time when the racial mixtures had crystallized into new peoples? Finally the supreme instance of a racial melting pot is the United States; that country is also one of the principal centres of contemporary civilization.

Accordingly we can sum up the position more or less as follows: (a) miscegenation has existed since the dawn of human life; (b) miscegenation results in a greater somatic and psychic variability and allows of the emergence of a great variety of new gene combinations, thus increasing the range of hereditary characteristics in the new population group; (c) speaking biologically, miscegenation is neither good nor bad, its effects being dependent in every case on the individual characteristics of the persons between whom such crossbreeding takes place. As, in general, miscegenation occurs more frequently between individuals on the lower social levels and in unsatisfactory economic and social circumstances, the causes of certain anomalies observable must be sought in this fact rather than in the fact of miscegenation as such; (d) examples of 'pure races' or of isolated human groups having developed a high culture independently are the exception; (e) on the contrary the great majority of areas of high civilization are inhabited by obviously cross-bred groups.

COLOUR PREJUDICE: THE NEGRO MYTH

So far as can be seen, few of the physical traits used for the classification of human races have functional value for the individuals displaying them. Our own civilization attaches special importance to the colour of the skin and relatively dark pigmentation is a mark of difference condemning numerous human groups to contempt, ostracism and a debased social status. In certain persons colour prejudice is so strong as to give rise to almost pathological phobias; these are not innate but reflect, in an exaggerated form, the prejudices of the social environment. To maintain that a man is an inferior human being because he is black is as ridiculous as contending that a white horse will necessarily be faster than a black horse. Nevertheless, however little basis there may be for colour prejudice, the importance of the resultant attitudes and behaviour in many countries is indisputable.

The exploitation by the whites of agriculture and mining in the newly-discovered countries from the fifteenth century onwards created slavery, particularly the enslavement of Negroes and American Indians. Simultaneously the pride of the white man and his superiority complex towards men of colour was increased and strengthened still further by the fact that he was a Christian whereas Negroes and Amerindians were pagans. In point of fact, however, the causes of white aggression were fundamentally economic; the whites seized the richer lands inhabited by coloured populations and reduced the latter to slavery to secure a ready source of labour which would increase the value of their recent acquisitions.

While it is true that we have in Las Casas a fierce champion of the abolition not only of Indian but of Negro slavery, 'because the same reasons apply in their case as in the Indians', there were more people who sought to maintain the *status quo* on the grounds that the Negro was 'inferior' to the white man. For instance, in 1772 the Reverend Thomas Thompson published a monograph, *The Trade in Negro Slaves on the African Coast in Accordance with Humane Principles and with the Laws of Revealed Religion,* in 1852 the Rev. Josiah Priest published *A Bible Defence of Slavery,* while C. Carroll (1900) in his work *The Negro as a Beast or In the Image of God* includes a chapter ('Biblical and Scientific Proofs that the Negro is not a Member of the Human Race') in which he asserts that 'all scientific research confirms his typically simian nature'.

The final division among themselves by the white men of colonial territories for exploitation and government in the last third of the nineteenth century (more particularly at the Conference of Berlin in 1884 for the division of the African continent among the European powers) afforded glaring proof

21

of their complete indifference to the legal and ethical point that none of them had the slightest right to dispose of any part of Africa and still less of the lives, goods and labour of its inhabitants.

Despite the proclamation in the Declaration of Independence of the United States of the equal rights of all men and the explicit provision of the Fifteenth Amendment 'that it shall be illegal to deny or restrict (those rights) in any state of the Union on the grounds of race, colour or former condition of slavery', despite the inclusion of equivalent provisions in the Constitutions of most countries and despite the solemn agreement to the same effect in Article 2 of the Universal Declaration of Human Rights signed by the United Nations on 10 December 1948, it is all too obvious in practice how widespread throughout the world is social, economic and political discrimination against Negroes in particular and coloured races in general, based mainly on false racial concepts.

One of the major absurdities of colour prejudice in the United States is the classification of anyone admitting to an African ancestor as a 'Negro' regardless of his physical appearance. The result is that in this case a 'Negro' is not a biological term but denotes membership of a particular cultural, economic and social group. Some 'Negroes' are indistinguishable from white men and pass themselves off as such to escape anti-Negro discrimination. The lack of logic in this attitude becomes still clearer if we reflect that if a person with the smallest proportion of 'Negro blood' can be classified as a Negro, it is just as logical and fair to classify everyone with one drop of 'white blood' as white.

It has been reckoned that the coloured races represent approximately three-fifths of the world's total population. Obviously so large a proportion of the human race can neither be regarded as a negligible quantity nor relegated to a secondary and subordinate status. There must be mutual respect; men must learn to live with one another, without fear, hatred or contempt, without the urge to exaggerate differences at the expense of similarities, but seeking to understand their true extent and importance. If this is not done Dubois' prophecy of 1920 may well be fulfilled that the 1914-18 war 'would be nothing to compare with the fight for freedom which black and brown and yellow men must and will make unless their oppression and humiliation and insult at the hands of the White World cease. The Dark World is going to submit to its present treatment just as long as it must and not one moment longer'. Another Negro leader, Marcus Garvey, has said much the same: 'The bloodiest war of all is yet to come when Europe will match its strength against Asia and that will be the Negro's opportunity to draw the sword for Africa's redemption.'

The greatest humiliations suffered by Negroes are social restrictions and personal insults: the exclusion of Negro travellers from certain trains and motor-coaches, the provision of restricted vehicles and waiting rooms, special schools, prohibited restaurants and hotels, etc., are to the Negro insulting and ridiculous. In South Africa, where colour prejudice is very strong, there was an instance in 1944 of certain officials being dismissed from their posts for refusal to obey Government instructions that the same courtesy terms should be used in official documents addressed to coloured persons as in those to whites.

It would appear that those most insistent on discrimination against Negroes are the lower class whites; they are the first to fear Negro competition in the economic field, and as they have no other argument to warrant their attitude of superiority towards Negroes, they rely on skin pigmentation to which they give an altogether exaggerated importance.

Colour prejudice has not only served as the basis for introducing a caste system in our society; it has also been used as a weapon by labour unions to combat competition by a black or yellow proletariat. The colour barriers raised by American, South African or Australian labour federations and unions, themselves subscribing to socialist ideals and setting themselves up as the defenders of the working class, throw a lurid light on the economic rivalries which are the real motives behind racial antagonisms and the myths evolved to justify them.

Assumptions about psychological and social characteristics based on the colour of the skin are not merely absurd but disingenuous, they vary with circumstances. As an example we may take the changes in the views held about the Japanese: in 1935 the majority of North Americans thought of them as 'progressive', 'intelligent', and 'industrious'; in 1942 they had become 'cunning', and 'treacherous'; in 1950 things have changed again. When there was a shortage of Chinese labourers in California they were described as 'frugal', 'sober' and 'law-abiding'; the moment competition became severe and it was necessary to exclude them, they were described as 'dirty', 'repulsive', 'unassimilable' and even 'dangerous'. The same lack of objective criteria might later be found in India: while North American troops described the natives as 'dirty', and 'uncivilized', the Hindu intellectuals described the Americans as 'boorish', 'materialistic', 'unintellectual' and 'uncivilized'.

Regarding the supposed inferiority of the Negro's psychosomatic attributes to those of the white man. Hankins claims that the bulk of the brain is less in the Negro and deducts that the Negro is mentally inferior. H. L. Gordon (1933) asserts that congenital cerebral deficiency is a characteristic of the Negroes of Kenya, resulting, in his view too, from the lesser cranial volume and the difference in conformation of the Negro brain.

In many instances the peculiar body odour of the Negro and his marked prognathism have been regarded as proof of his biological inferiority. However, it is above all in the psychological field that the most sustained effort has been made to prove the superiority of the white man over the Negro. Admittedly Negro and white are in no respect identical either physically, intellectually or emotionally; nevertheless this does not warrant the assertion that the differences imply any superiority of the one over the other.

The investigations of Leaky in Africa and Steggerda among the Negroes of Jamaica have shown that their cranial capacity is not inferior, and even superior in some cases, to that of the white man. This is confirmed by the work of J. Huxley and A. Keith. For further confirmation of this view we may turn to the work of J. H. F. Kohlbrugge (1935) on the formation of the brain, based on earlier research by such eminent anthropologists and doctors as Reezius, Weinberg, Sergi and Kappers. He draws the following important conclusions:

1. The weight of the frontal lobe, regarded as the seat of the intellect, is 44 per cent of the total weight of the brain in men and women, *black and white alike*.
2. No racial differences are observable as regards the weight of the brain; there are however, marked variations between individuals within each human group or 'race'.
3. Men of marked intellectual powers have not necessarily possessed brains greater in weight or volume.
4. Comparison of the incisures and convolutions of the brain afford equally little support for the view that there are discernible differences between the races; *all* variations are found in *all* 'races'. The writer concludes: 'If the specimens available were mixed up there is no one who could dis-

tinguish the brains of Australians from those of Europeans nor those of people of high intelligence from average brains.'

The work of Sergi on Negroes and Kappers on Chinese confirms these important conclusions, which explode the unwarranted assertion *that the presumed* intellectual inferiority of the Negro is due to the (*presumed and arbitrary*) fact of the brains of coloured races being smaller in volume and less complex structurally.

Admitted the prognathism frequently found in Negroes is a primitive somatic trait. However, the lack of body hair, the thickness of the lips, and the texture of the hair of the head, etc., are all consistent with a more advanced stage of evolution in the Negro than in the white man. We can say with Ruth Benedict that 'No race has an exclusive claim to represent the final stage in human evolution; there is no valid argument to confirm that certain selected traits may indicate the superiority of the white race'.

In this connexion the terms 'good', 'bad', 'superior' and 'inferior' are meaningless as they are all subjective terms; in every case they should be used in a specific connexion, e.g.: 'the majority of Negroes are superior to white people in their resistance to malaria'; or 'the majority of white people are superior to the majority of Negroes in resistance to tuberculosis', etc. The result would be to show that every human group is superior in some respects and inferior in others.

In comparisons of the position of the white and Negro races today there is a tendency to assume the inferiority of the latter from the fact that their economic, political and cultural evolution is far behind that of the whites. This, however, is not due to an 'innate racial inferiority', but is purely the result of circumstances and due to the régime of exploitation under which almost all Negroes live today as a result of white colonization and of the existence, if not of slavery in law, of conditions equivalent to it in practice.

Too often the Negro is still in a position of economic semi-slavery, he is enmeshed in a network of restrictions, partly legal and partly not. Poverty, contempt and disease have made him what he is today.

Regarding the supposed laziness of the Negro (as also of the American Indian) the cause may well be lack of incentive. As Burns rightly points out, the vast yield of the West African colonies, where some land is still in Negro hands, shows that the Negro is not lazy by nature. When he is interested in and

25

understands his work he will expend energy without stint, but he wants to select his own hours of work without feeling himself the prisoner of the time-recorder. Similarly the Amerindian, in a position to till his own land and secure the full fruit of his endeavours, undoubtedly works with a degree of energy, enthusiasm and efficiency unknown in cases where he is aware that it is the 'boss' who will draw the profit. Booker Washington holds that the greatest harm inflicted on the Negro by slavery was to deprive him of the sense of personal independence, method and the spirit of initiative.

There is no reason why whites and Negroes should not dwell together amicably as fellow citizens of a country and of the world, why they should not show mutual consideration and respect without either group having to sacrifice anything of its individuality, in just the same way as Catholics and Protestants in many countries can remain on excellent terms without slackening their religious standards.

What offends Negroes is their systematic exclusion on grounds of colour from certain social facilities open to white men of very doubtful culture and education. It is the general attitude of white people towards them, the lack of consideration and the deliberate slights which make them desire increasingly every day to be delivered from this everlasting ostracism and from the degradation which brands them as almost members of another species, as sub-human (Mathews, quoted by Burns).

There are Negroes whose quite understandable inferiority complex leads them to read hostility to their race, and the wish to keep them down, into any painful or even disagreeable action or decision, even when it relates to an individual only and colour prejudice does not enter into it in the slightest degree. The seething rancour and hatred born of past offences, the mistrust of advances by white people, the bitter and sometimes overt loathing of everything white, must all be conquered, subdued and forgotten if a real spirit of understanding is to grow up between the two races.

At various points in history religious wars put an end to all tolerance in religion. The writer believes that war between the races can be prevented if white people throughout the world stop inflicting on the Negro slights, oppression and injustice, and adopt a civilized and decent attitude towards coloured peoples distinguished by tolerance and good neighbourliness. We must make it impossible for any coloured man to say, as a Hawaian did to a missionary: 'When the white man came you had the Bible and we owned the land; now we have the Bible and you have the land.'

The contributions of Negroes as a race or as individuals to world civilization are not an adequate basis for prognostication of what the race may be able to achieve in the future in terms of its own aptitudes and under more satisfactory environmental, social and economic conditions. Moreover, we must not forget that the twelfth century Negro university of Timbuctoo could stand comparison with European schools and the same is true as regards the respective levels of civilization in Europe and in the three great Negro kingdoms of the age. Moreover, it is quite possible that the working of iron, which is fundamental to all modern technology, was a Negro discovery. Lord Olivier (1905) has said truly, 'the Negro is progressing and that disposes of all the arguments in the world that he is incapable of progress'.

To sum up, all the evidence of biology, anthropology, evolution and genetics demonstrates that racial discrimination on grounds of colour is a myth without the slightest scientific warrant, and hence that the supposed 'racial inferiority of coloured peoples' is untrue. It is unfavourable environmental, political and social-economic factors which alone keep these groups at their present level.

THE JEWISH MYTH

Jews are a human group which have aroused deep hatred in almost all countries and almost all ages.

Anti-Semitism, as a social and political attitude, infecting whole States in some instances and extensive sectors of the population in others, and defended to a greater or lesser extent on religious and economic grounds, is a long-standing antagonism of which examples are found far back in history. To indicate its persistence, we may quote such instances as the mass expulsion of the Jews from Spain in the fifteenth century, the segregation of Jews in Christian Europe during the Middle Ages, the Dreyfus case in France, the notorious pogroms of Jews at various times and in various parts of Eastern and Central Europe, and the use for world-wide propaganda of the spurious 'Protocols of the Learned Elders of Zion', with which it was sought to exacerbate anti-Semitic feeling among the masses.

Today, however, anti-Semitism has resorted to the *myth of a Jewish race* in an attempt to justify itself and to provide a pseudo-scientific cloak for its political and economic motives. The type regarded as typically 'Jewish' is actually very common among the peoples of the Levant and the Near East, though most of these peoples are not Jews and never have been, either in religion or in other aspects of their culture.

The fact that some Jews can be identified as such on sight is due less to inherited physical traits than to the conditioning of emotional and other reactions productive of distinctive facial expressions and corporal attitudes, mannerisms, intonation and tendencies of temperament and character, by Jewish custom and the treatment inflicted on Jews by non-Jews.

If the Nazis had had genuine distinctive 'Jewish' characteristics to go on, why were Jews obliged to display the Star of David on their clothing to allow of their identification by Aryans?

As far as Italy is concerned, Mussolini said in 1932: 'There are no pure races and there is no anti-Semitism in Italy. Italian Jews have always behaved well as citizens and have fought valiantly as soldiers.'

In 1936 the German-Italian alliance forced him to begin an anti-Jewish campaign, although the more obvious heterogeneity of the Italian people resulted in Italian racism differing from German. The Fascist manifesto of 14 July 1938 proclaims: 'There is a pure Italian race. The question of race in Italy should be dealt with from a purely biological angle independently of philosophical or religious considerations. The concept of race in Italy must be essentially Italian and Aryan-Nordic. . . . Jews do not belong to the Italian race. Of the Semites who have settled throughout the centuries on the sacred soil of our fatherland, it is generally true to say that none has remained there. Even the Arab occupation of Sicily has left no traces save the memorial of a few names.' This Fascist claim that there exists in Italy a pure Italian race of Aryan-Nordic type would be laughable if it were not tragic. The principal point the writer wishes to stress is that the anti-Semitic attitude of Italian Fascism is a clumsy imitation of Nazism, thus, like it, based on false biological premises.

What are the alleged anthropological characteristics distinguishing the Jewish race?

The Jews were a nation until the taking of Jerusalem by Titus in A.D. 70. At the beginning of the Christian era and

28

perhaps earlier, there was emigration of Jews from Palestine to various countries from which, in many instances, they were later expelled, thus giving rise to what might be called secondary migrations and population movements. It would be interesting to know the racial characteristics of the Hebrews of antiquity who are probably the main ancestors of the Jews of today; so far, however, it has not been possible to ascertain them and thus it becomes necessary to conduct the investigation along other lines.

At a very early date, the Semites interbred with such neighbouring peoples of western Asia as Canaanites, Philistines, Arabs, Hittites, etc., and thus, even if the Hebrews were originally a pure race, there had been extensive crossing with several other races even in antiquity.

In addition to the new State of Israel, there are extensive Jewish colonies in Asia such as those in Transcaucasia, Syria, Mesopotamia, the Yemen (Arabia), Samarcand, Bokhara (Turkistan), Iran, Herat (Afghanistan), etc.

Jewish settlement in North Africa (Morocco and Algiers) began in 1000 B.C. and there were further settlements later. Three distinct types are found in this part of the world, reflecting distinctive ancestral origins: (a) Jews of the old stock, now few in number, who frequently present the classical Hebrew traits of light complexion, dark hair and eyes and large hooked nose; (b) Jews in whom Spanish characteristics predominate; (c) Jews of the Arab-Berber type: these are the most numerous and are barely distinguishable from the native peoples among whom they live. Thus while some Jewish communities in Africa resemble each other in somatic characteristics, others bear a much closer resemblance to Asiatic peoples.

In Spain there was an important Jewish colony from the beginning of the Christian era. On their expulsion in 1492, the Spanish Jews scattered to North Africa, the Balkans and Russia. Jews of Spanish origin are dolichocephalic whereas Russian Jews are brachycephalic, a difference explainable by the fact that the skull conformation of each group resembles that of the Spanish and Russian populations among which they live. A similar general observation may be made regarding the Jews of Poland, Germany and Austria. Of English Jews, 28.3 per cent are dolichocephalic, 24.3 per cent mesocephalic and 47.4 per cent brachycephalic, whereas of the Jewish population of Daghestan (Caucasus), 5 per cent are dolichocephalic, 10 per cent mesaticephalic and 85 per cent brachycephalic.

With respect to cranial conformation, it may be said, generally speaking, that in Asia the predominant type is brachycephalic, though there are some dolichocephalic groups; in Africa the predominance of the dolichocephalic group is absolute; while Europe contains both dolichocephalics (more particularly stocks of Spanish origin), mesaticephalics and brachycephalics. It is not possible in the present paper to quote the detailed statistics proving the variability of all the other somatic characteristics in the misnamed 'Jewish Race'; however, it may be mentioned that 49 per cent of Polish Jews are light haired and 51 per cent dark haired, while there are only 32 per cent of blonds among German Jews. Thirty per cent of the Jews of Vienna have light coloured eyes. The hooked nose, which seems so typically Jewish, occurs in 44 per cent only of the individuals of certain groups while straight noses are found in 40 per cent, the so-called 'roman' nose in 9 per cent and tip-tilted in 7 per cent.

All the above is clear proof of the variability and lack of morphological unity of the Jewish peoples. In confirmation of this view R. N. Salaman says: 'The purity of the Jewish race is imaginary; the widest variety of ethnic types is found among Jews ranging, as regard cranial conformation only, from brachycephalics to hyperdolichocephalics. More particularly in Germany and Russia, there are Jews who do not display the smallest Semitic characteristic.'

Fishberg adds: 'The percentage of light-eyed blonds and their irregular distribution in the various centres of Jewish population, the extreme variability of the cranial index—at least as great as that observable between any of the peoples of Europe the existence among Jews of negroid, mongoloid and teutonic types, the variations in stature, etc., are other proofs of the non-existence of one Semitic race unmodified since biblical times. Hence the claims of Jews to purity of descent are as vain and baseless as the allegations of a radical difference between Jews and the so-called Aryan race on which anti-Semitism is based.'

The Jews who emigrated from their country of origin at various times in history were crossbreeds to a degree varying directly with the date of emigration. On arriving in the new country, some of the settlers married among themselves and thus perpetuated the original cross, but far more frequently they interbred with the aborigines. This is not mere supposition for there are facts to prove it, despite the widespread belief that the Jews keep themselves apart:

1. From very early in the Christian era numerous laws were promulgated prohibiting marriage between orthodox Christians and Jews, e.g., the codex of Theodosius II in the sixth century; the Council of Orleans in 538; the laws issued by the ecclesiastical authorities in Toledo in 589, in Rome in 743, and by King Ladislas II of Hungary in 1092. The fact that such prohibitions were necessary suggests that unions between Jews and Christians were frequent. Spielmann quotes numerous instances of marriages between Germans and Jews which resulted in the partners being deported by the Merovingian king to different cities of the Rhineland.

2. It is calculated that in Germany, between 1921 and 1925, for every 100 Jewish marriages, there were 58 all-Jewish and 42 mixed. In Berlin, in 1926, there were 861 all-Jewish marriages and 554 mixed. The figures speak for themselves, especially if we take into account the large number of partners who became Jews by religion although there was nothing 'Semitic' about them.

3. It is obvious that all Jewish communities are of mixed stock whatever the country in which they reside, since, even if they were segregated at certain epochs, these measures could never be strictly, nor for long, maintained or complied with. This is so far true that the general analysis and classification of Jews according to origin gives us the following separate groups: (a) descendants of Jewish emigrants from Palestine (very few); (b) descendants of unions between Jews of mixed Asiatic descent or between Jews and other groups, who might be called cross-crossbreeds; (c) Jews by religion but having anthropologically no connexion whatever with the Jews of Palestine and consisting simply of individuals of other human strains converted to the Hebrew religion. A typical example of this class is Boulan, King of the Khazars, converted to Judaism in 740 with many of his nobles and peoples; there are still numerous Jews in Poland and South Russia tracing their descent from this group.

Thus despite the view usually held, the Jewish people is racially heterogeneous; its constant migrations and its relations—voluntary or otherwise—with the widest variety of nations and peoples have brought about such a degree of crossbreeding that *the so-called people of Israel can produce examples of traits typical of every people.* For proof it will suffice to compare the rubicund, sturdy, heavily-built Rotter-

dam Jew with his co-religionist, say, in Salonika with gleam-
ing eyes in a sickly face and skinny, high-strung physique.
Hence, so far as our knowledge now goes, we can assert that
Jews as a whole display as great a degree of morphological
disparity among themselves as could be found between members of two or more different races.

This raises a problem: if, scientifically speaking, it can
readily be demonstrated that the Jewish people is heterogeneous and that there is no such thing as a Jewish race, how
is it that in fact some Jews can almost infallibly be identified
as such at first glance? The probable explanation is that the
Jews in question are those who retain certain ancestral Jewish
characteristics: aquiline nose, pale skin in combination with
dark eyes and hair. Nevertheless, we fail to notice and identify a much larger number of Jews who have taken on the
traits of the people among whom they live and thus pass
unnoticed.

Another point is that individuals professing the same religion attain a degree of similarity in gestures, habits, dress, etc.,
which facilitates their identification. Among the Jews, whose
rites and customs are extremely rigid, this outward similarity
arising from their ethnographic, linguistic and religious affi-
nities is strongly marked though quite unconnected with the
variety of morphological types making up that people.

There is therefore no foundation for the claim that there is
a Jewish race; it is a biological *myth* affording no valid basis
for an anti-Semitic attitude.

THE MYTH OF 'ARYAN' OR 'NORDIC' SUPERIORITY

Racists were not content with proclaiming the 'superiority'
of white over coloured races nor with discriminating against
Jews nor even with combating miscegenation and asserting
a priori that it was dangerous as leading to racial degeneration.
They also felt it necessary to erect biological and psychological hierarchies within the white race itself in an attempt
to justify new rights of conquest, domination and overlord-
ship vested in a still more exclusive caste.

That is the origin of 'Aryanism' or 'Nordicism' as a basic
doctrine of racial superiority. The Aryan myth is the common source of other secondary myths—Germanism, Anglo-

Saxonism, and Celticism, evolved concurrently in Germany, England, the United States and France.

Let us consider the origin, distribution and essential characteristics of the superior 'Aryan' type.

ORIGIN OF THE ARYANS

The philological similarities between Sanskrit, Greek, Latin, German and the Celtic tongues observed by W. Jones (1788) led Thomas Young (1813) to adopt the term 'Indo-European' to designate the common root of these and other languages. The view quickly gained currency that there had been an Indo-European people and J. G. Rhode (1820) located their original home in Central Asia. Later J. von Kalproth suggested that the term 'Indo-European' be replaced by 'Indo-Germanic', a term whose use was made fairly general by the works of Prichard (1831) and F. Bopp (1833). In 1840 F. A. Pott suggested the valleys of the Oxus and Iaxarte and the slopes of the Hindu Kush as the home of the primitive Aryan people; though without any solid basis, this hypothesis was accepted until the end of the nineteenth century.

With Max Müller (1861), belief in the Asiatic origin of the Aryans became very widespread; Müller repeatedly stressed the desirability of replacing the terms 'Indo-Germanic' and 'Indo-European' by 'Aryan' on the grounds that the people which invaded India and whose language was Sanskrit called itself *Arya*. According to Müller the primitive Aryan language implied the existence of an 'Aryan race' which was the common ancestor of Hindus, Persians, Greeks, Romans, Slavs, Celts and Germans. Later, however, he reacted against the notion of 'racial' Aryanism and, as we shall see later, reverted to the view that it was a purely linguistic term.

J. J. d'Omalius d'Halloy (1848-64), R. T. Latham (1862), Bulwer Lytton (1842), Adolphe Pictet (1859-64) and others denied the alleged Asiatic origin of the Indo-Europeans. Benfey (1868) held that the Aryans came from the northern shores of the Black Sea between the Danube and the Caspian. Louis Leiger (1870) located them on the south shore of the Baltic and J. G. Cunok (1871) in the area between the North Sea and the Urals. D. G. Brinton (1890) believed the original home of the Aryans to have been West Africa while K. F. Johanson (around 1900) took the view that the waves of Aryan emigration had spread outwards from the Baltic. Peter

Giles (1922) thought they came from the plains of Hungary. V. Gordon Childe (1892) argued for south Russia as their place of origin, while G. Kossina (1921) believed them to have come from northern Europe. At the same time there were others such as R. Hartmann (1876), G. de Mortillet (1866) and Houzé (1906) who maintained that the Aryans were no more than a figment of certain writers' imagination, 'begotten in the study'.

The examples quoted demonstrate the variety of opinions held on the subject—opinions which in many cases flatly contradict each other. This must bring us to the conviction that the existence of the so-called Aryan 'people' or 'race' is a mere myth since we find purely subjective criteria employed in the attempt to determine its home, without the slightest factual and scientific foundation.

DOCTRINE OF. ARYANISM AND TEUTONISM

The first to propound the theory of an aristocracy of 'German blood' was Count Henri de Boullainvillers (1658-1722), but it was Arthur de Gobineau who laid down the doctrine of 'Aryanism' in all its fullness (*Essai sur l'inégalité des races humaines,* 1853) and proclaimed the superiority of the 'Aryan race' over the other white strains. His ideas had a considerable influence on philosophical and political thought in Europe and from the first he was well known in Germany, where he made contact with Richard Wagner who helped to spread his ideas. However, it was only later that his theory exercised any influence or achieved any degree of acceptance in France, his native country.

Gobineau was the descendant of a burgher family of the seventeenth century who wished to prove the nobility of his family's origin, and his work is primarily the result of research designed to demonstrate the 'superiority' of his own caste. Hence Gobineau's racism is not a *nationalist* but a *class* concept of aristocracy, to defend the latter's position against a bastard proletariat. His 'Aryan' race was a 'superior' caste, the pure-bred, select and privileged minority born to govern and direct the destinies of the 'inferior' crossbred masses in any nation. Gobineau was neither pro-French nor pro-German; he merely asserted the 'superior pure Aryan descent of the aristocracy' in whatever country.

It was after the Franco-Prussian war of 1870 that 'Aryanism' as a doctrine proclaiming the innate superiority of a social class became transformed into a dogma of 'the superiority of certain nations'. While it was erroneous—as we shall see—to postulate the biological purity of a social class, it was a still greater absurdity to assert the racial purity of a nation. Nevertheless among the French, the Germans and the Anglo-Saxons alike, men of letters, politicians and pseudo-scientists were found to devote their energies to demonstrating that the triumphs of civilization were due exclusively to their own respective 'races'. The champions of Aryanism lauded the Nordic element as the source of all higher civilizations and major achievements of humanity in whatever age and place. In Gobineau's view, for instance, the Chinese civilization arose as a result of the infiltration of 'Aryan blood'.

Gobineau is not very definite as to the characteristics or traits of 'Aryans'. They may be brachycephalic or dolichocephalic; the eyes are usually light in colour, but may be dark or even black (it should be remembered that he himself was a dark-eyed Frenchman). It is his followers who ascribe to the exclusively 'Aryan' type, tallness, blue eyes, fair hair and long heads with the following psychic qualities as well: virility; innate nobility; natural aggressiveness; imperturbable objectivity; dislike of useless words and vain rhetoric; distaste for the amorphous mass; precise intelligence; the spirit of independence; sternness to themselves and others; well-developed sense of responsibility; great foresight; tenacity of will; the qualities of a race of leaders, men of great undertakings and large and well-thought-out ideas, etc.

Houston Stewart Chamberlain (1899), a pro-German Englishman and son-in-law of Richard Wagner, was the keenest supporter of the racist theory of the 'blond, dolichocephalic Nordic'; he adopted the terms 'Teutonic race' and 'Teuton blood', thus giving a frankly nationalist twist to Gobineau's class thesis. Assuming that the 'blond German' has a God-given mission to fulfil and that 'the Teutons are the aristocracy of humanity', whereas 'Latins are a degenerate population group', the conclusion drawn is that European civilization, even in countries classed as Slavonic and Latin, is the work of 'the Teuton race': e.g., Greece, Rome, the Papacy, the Renaissance, the French Revolution and the Napoleonic Empire. He goes on to assert: 'where the Germanic element has not penetrated, there is no civilization in our sense'.

Let us examine a few examples of this fantastic theory. The

'Aryan Greeks' were successful in the arts, but lacked the spirit of political organization as a result of miscegenation between their race and the Semitic, the latter containing a proportion of black blood. By the same process of imagination run mad, Julius Caesar, Alexander the Great, Leonardo da Vinci, Galileo, Voltaire, Marco Polo, Roger Bacon, Giotto, Galvani, Lavoisier, Watt and many others are all claimed as Teutons and Napoleon himself is regarded as probably descended from the Vandals.

Other great figures in history are described as products of the mixture of 'Teuton blood' with the 'dark southern race'; this class includes such men as Dante, Raphael, Michelangelo and Shakespeare, who are described as 'men of genius, not on account of, but in spite of their mixed blood'; 'their natural gifts represent the heritage received from the Teutonic race'. Referring to the apostle Paul, whom they seek to include in the 'Aryan group', writers of this school conclude that so great a man could not be a 'pure blooded' Jew and accordingly they purport to discover that he was the son of a Jewish father and a Greek mother. Of Jesus, Waltmann says: 'There is not the slightest proof that his parents were of Jewish descent; there is no doubt that the Galileans had a proportion of Aryan blood: moreover, Christ's Aryanism is obvious in his Message', furthermore, 'Joseph was not his father, because Jesus had no father'. Nevertheless, when Hitlerian Nazism clashed with the Church, no racial theorist any longer dared to refer to the 'Aryan' origin of St. Paul and of Jesus Christ.

Exaltation of the Teutonic race reaches its final pitch of absurdity in Waltmann's assertion on the strength of imaginary philological homologies of the Germanic origin of other great figures of the Renaissance: e.g., Giotto, formerly Jothe; Alighieri, formerly Aigler; Vinci, formerly Wincke; Tasso, formerly Dasse; Buonarotti Michelangelo, formerly Bohurodt; Velazquez, formerly Velahise; Murillo, formerly Moerl; Diderot, formerly Tietroh, etc.

ANTHROPOSOCIOLOGY AND SOCIAL SELECTION

This school of thought, introduced by G. Vacher de Lapouge (1896) in France and Otto Ammon (1898) in Germany, is a special variant of 'racial determinism' based on statistical researches of considerable interest in themselves, but whose results were interpreted in conformity with the preconceived idea of 'the superiority of the blond dolichocephalic type'. As a result of his examination of seventeenth and eighteenth century skulls in Montpellier, de Lapouge thought he could prove that members of higher social classes had a lower cephalic index than the common people, i.e., the latter's skulls were rounder or brachycephalic.

Certain of his conclusions may be summed up as follows:

1. In countries of mixed blood, wealth increases in inverse ratio to the cephalic index; i.e. individuals with a lower cephalic index (dolichocephalics) are the richer.
2. City-dwellers are predominantly dolichocephalic whereas brachycephalics are dominant in rural areas.
3. Urban life exercises a selective influence unfavourable to brachycephalic elements.
4. There is a greater tendency to dolichocephalism in the higher than in the lower classes; competition for the higher social positions tends to eliminate brachycephalics, who are more frequently found among workmen.
5. Since prehistoric times there has been a steady increase in the cephalic index in Europe. De Lapouge accordingly forecast the extinction of the 'blond dolichocephalic' and hence a subsequent Dark Age in the world.

All the above hypotheses are based simply and solely on the so-called Ammon's Law which asserts the concentration of dolichocephalics in the city and their social 'superiority' to brachycephalics.

The work of Levi in Italy (1896), Oloriz in Spain (1894), Beddoe in England (1905) and Houzé in Belgium (1906) demonstrated the falsity not only of Ammon's Law but also of the over-hasty deductions made by its supporters. There is no doubt that according to statistics for Germany and northern Italy students (representing the higher social classes) were predominantly dolichocephalic; however, the opposite is the case in southern Italy. Furthermore, anthroposociologists themselves reckoned that the Mediterranean dolichocephalic type was 'inferior' to the brachycephalic Alpine, whereas their own theory should have led them to accept the Negro, the most dolichocephalic type in the world, as one of the 'superior' peoples. Furthermore, Ammon draws attention to instances of brachycephaly and dark complexion among intellectuals, and to explain it away writes: 'a slight admixture of brachycephalic blood is advantageous as it tends to modify the excessive ardour of the Aryan and gives them

37

the spirit of perseverance and reflexion which makes them better fitted for scientific studies'; 'instances are found of people of true Germanic type as regards colour of skin, eyes and hair but brachycephalic and hence psychologically of the brachycephalic type'; 'skull formation is however the important point as it determines the shape of the brain and hence the psychological type'. Vacher de Lapouge went so far as to assert that 'a brachycephalic skull is evidence of total incapacity in the individuals concerned to raise themselves above barbarism'.

However, statistical research, including that of de Lapouge and Ammon themselves, showed that (contrary to their assertions) there was a tendency to brachycephaly in intellectuals and even a preponderance of dark complexioned types among the so-called superior classes. Accordingly de Lapouge took refuge in another sophistry and labelled intellectuals 'false brachycephalics', an expression devoid of the slightest anthropological meaning.

In fact somatic study of people classed as intellectuals in the different countries would show the utmost variety of combinations of the anthropological traits attributed to the different so-called primitive races.

We accordingly see that the theories and data put forward by anthroposociologists are obviously contradictory and prove nothing as to the alleged 'intellectual superiority of the dolichocephalics'. Nor have they been able to confirm that the alleged selective influence of the great cities on newcomers operates according to the shape of the skull, and even less that the proportion of dolichocephalics is higher in the 'superior classes'.

Anthroposociology believed in and preached the superiority of dolichocephalic blonds, but all it really achieved was to reinforce powerfully the racial arrogance of self-styled 'Aryans' and to increase the aggressive tendencies of Teuton and Pan-German chauvinism by giving it the false illusion of having ethical warrant.

THE 'ARYAN' THESIS OF CONTEMPORARY NAZISM AND FASCISM

The nationalist application of 'Aryan racism' in H. S. Chamberlain, Waltmann, Theodor Pesche, Karl Penca, and Richard Wagner found convinced adherents, who played a powerful part as propagandists and caused the hypothesis of the supremacy of the 'Aryan' or 'Teuton' race to take root in Germany. In 1894, belief in the God-ordained superiority of Germany became a quasi-religious cult with the foundation in Freiburg, under the chairmanship of L. Schemann, of the 'Gobineau Vereinigung'. Hence, the doctrines of 'race purity' and 'race superiority' attained much greater importance in Germany than elsewhere, and finally became articles of faith, dangerous by the time of the first world war. While the German leaders stirred up the popular frenzy for the defence of Teutonic culture and its propagation among the other 'less civilized' races of Europe, these in their turn alleged that the German 'blonds' were not Europeans but of Asiatic origin and descendants of the Huns, lacking all the elements of true culture, without the smallest notion of the concept of liberty and democracy, and deserving extermination to the last man.

In connexion with the non-existence of the 'Aryan' or 'Nordic' type, there is an historical anecdote worthy of recollection. Before 1914, William II wished a racial map of Germany to be produced displaying the incidence of the 'Aryan' element; however, the data assembled could not be published since heterogeneity was so marked, and in whole regions such as Baden there were no Nordics.

The post-war period (1919-39) did nothing to improve relations between the peoples and the Aryan racist myth again served political ends, those of the Nazis and Fascists. J. L. Reimer (*Ein Pangermanisches Deutschland*) even proposed the establishment of a system of castes based on the varying proportion of 'German blood': (a) an upper caste of 'pure-blooded' Germans, 'ideal Teutons', to enjoy full political and social privileges; (b) an intermediate caste of 'partly German' blood to have restricted privileges only; (c) a caste of non-Germans deprived of all political rights who should be sterilized so as to safeguard the State and the future of civilization.

One of the theorists of Hitlerite racism, F. K. Günther (1920-37) has described the Alpine type as psychologically 'specially fitted to end up as the muddle-headed owner of a cottage and a patch of garden', while the Alpine woman will turn into a 'faded little creature growing old in a debased and narrow world'; Alpines according to him are 'petty criminals, small-time swindlers, sneak-thieves and sexual perverts'. Nordics on the other hand are 'capable of the nobler crimes'. However, there are racist fanatics even wilder than Günther; according to Gauch (*Neue Grundlagen der Rassenforschung*, 1933), the difference in anatomical and histological structure (hair, bones, teeth and tegument) between man and animals, is *less* than that between Nordics and other human races; only Nordics possess perfect articulate speech; only in Nordics do we find the correct biped position, etc. He ends by suggesting that a strict line should be drawn between 'Nordic' man and the animal world, the latter comprising all non-Nordic humanity.

Hitler himself (*Mein Kampf*, 1925), on the question of German superiority writes: 'It is outstandingly evident from history that when the Aryan has mixed his blood with that of the inferior peoples, the result of the miscegenation has invariably been the ruin of the civilizing races. In the United States where a vast majority of the population consists of German elements among whom there has only been a small degree of interbreeding with inferior peoples belonging to the coloured races, both the human population and the civilization are different from their counterparts in Central and South America where the bulk of the immigrants have interbred with the aborigines . . .'; 'The German who has maintained his racial purity without interbreeding has become the *master* of the American continent and will continue to be its master as long as he does not commit suicide in his turn by an incestuous contamination.' In other words the Latin-American—according to German racists—is predestined to irremediable biological degeneration and hence to live under the rule of the pure Aryan' or 'German' race. Comment is needless.

In the previous chapter we pointed out that Italian Fascism not only proclaimed its anti-Semitism but also its 'Nordic' racism as the basis of national unity and of political and economic alliance with Nazism.

America itself is not free of this aberration and can show genuinely racist authors such as Madison Grant (*Passing of the Great Race*, 1916), Clinton B. Stoddard (*America's Race Heritage*, 1922) and Lothrop Stoddard (*The Revolt against Civilization; The Menace of the Underman*, 1922) who maintain and propagate their standard of 'Nordic superiority' with such statements as these: 'The proportion of Nordic blood in each nation is an exact measure of its power in war and its place in civilization'; 'The Nordic element in France decayed and with it the country's strength'; 'The superstition and lack of intelligence of the Spaniard of today is due to the replacement of the Nordic element by Alpine and Mediterranean strains, etc.'

40

THE ALLEGED 'ANGLO-SAXON' TYPE

The alleged somatic uniformity of the *Anglo-Saxon* race can be exploded as readily. If North Americans were direct descendants of the Pilgrim Fathers, and if England at that period could be deemed an exclusively Anglo-Saxon country, there might be some basis for the thesis of this type's 'purity'. It has been said that 'the Teutonic invaders exterminated all the native inhabitants of England in a glorious universal slaughter'. The truth is, however, that the Teuton conquerors were no more than a new element in the racial complex of the British Isles, and they themselves were very far from being morphologically homogeneous.

As far as the United States are concerned, there is no doubt whatsoever that the original settlers in New England were drawn from many different strata of English society and accordingly presented great physical differences among themselves. Stature and the cephalic index alike show a considerable degree of variability in the English people and Parson (1920) proved statistically that while just under 25 per cent presented the combination of dark eyes and brown or black hair, those combining light eyes and blond hair were no more than 20 per cent; and that the most frequent combination was light eyes and dark hair, though there were individuals with dark eyes and blond hair. No evidence is to be found in the British Isles, and *a fortiori* even less in the United States, to justify the alleged identification of the 'Anglo-Saxon' race with either nation.

'CELTICISM'

Celticism, another variant of 'Aryanism', is one of the fruits of the strong nationalist tendency which developed in France after the war of 1870. It is asserted that it is the Celtic type which inhabits France and distinctive somato-psychic characteristics are ascribed to it which make it 'superior' to the rest of the white races. Whereas Gobineau, de Lapouge, Ammon, Chamberlain, Waltmann, etc., attribute the creative genius of France to the 'Aryan' and 'Teutonic' element, Celticism presents equally valid arguments for the 'racial superiority of the Celt'.

A. de Quatrefages (*La race prussienne*, 1872) holds that the racial descent of the Prussians is entirely different from that of the French and concludes: 'There is nothing Aryan about the Prussians'. In 1871 Broca affirmed that France was a nation of brachycephalic (Alpine) Gauls and maintained the superiority of that strain over the dolichocephalic German 'Nordic'. Isaac Tylor (*The Origin of the Aryans, 1890*), was another scientist who held that the Celts were a tall, brachycephalic race and the only Aryans.

The ambiguous use of terms and the confusion as to somatic characterization grow still greater when an attempt is made to define the Celt and the Gaul. Joseph Widney (1907) speaks of two Celtic types, the first tall, blond and dolichocephalic (like the Highland Scot and the people of Northern Ireland), the second short, dark and brachycephalic (like the Southern Irish). He regards the first as the true Celt, while the second is descended from a more ancient conquered race and has merely adopted the 'Celtic tongue'. However, he continues: 'The Celt has never maintained his blood unmixed'; 'the fatal propensity of the Celt to miscegenation has brought about the ruin of his race'. Widney claims that the blond dolichocephalic Celt is the dominant element in France; in France itself, however, the tendency is more to identify the Celt with the brachycephalic Alpine of intermediate stature and complexion.

Some schools of thought in France regard it as peopled by Celts, others by Gauls, though there is no agreement between French scholars as to which was which, nor whether they were or were not in fact the same race. Hence certain investigators hold that 'Celt' is a historical term of little scientific precision used to designate peoples speaking related languages and presenting every morphological variety from short, dark dolichocephalics through moderately fair brachycephalics of medium height to tall, blond, dolichocephalics. However, these entirely correct observations have little influence on a mentality imbued with 'racism'.

Whatever the 'Celtic' type may be, the fact is that between 2000 B.C. (end of the Neolithic Age in France) and the Teutonic migrations in the fifth century of our own era, very little is know about racial mixtures in western Europe. It seems fairly certain that there were successive waves of brachycephalic Alpine types or peoples in which that type preponderated. Like Germany and northern Italy, France was the meeting point of the three main races of Europe, as well as of any surviving palaeolithic groups: (a) the Mediterranean race was the indigenous stock in southern France, where it is still predominant; (b) Alpines penetrated towards the north-west and today constitute the bulk of the population of Savoy, Auvergne and Brittany; (c) the Nordic or Baltic races (Normans, Teutons, Saxons, Franks and Burgundians), all of whom were of extremely mixed stock, spread over France from north to south and one of them gave its name to the country. Even today the Germanic element predominates in extensive areas of northern France. To sum up, if we take into account the shape of the skull, colour of eyes, hair and skin and stature, it becomes evident that morphologically the French people was and is amazingly heterogeneous.

CRITICISM AND REFUTATION OF THESE THEORIES

The fundamental error of 'Aryanism' or 'Nordicism' in all its forms lies in a confusion of ideas which is very wide-spread but by any reckoning unscientific: the term *race* is used indifferently as a synonym for *language* and *nation*.

It has already been pointed out that the term 'race' has an exclusively biological significance. Nevertheless, the terms 'Latin race', 'Slav race', 'German race' and of course 'Aryan race' are in common use, and thus men fall into the error or regarding human groups which are only linguistically homogeneous as anthropologically uniform. In 1900 Havet wrote: 'Language and race are two entirely different concepts. In a discussion of linguistics not a single anthropological term should ever be used and similarly in anthropological studies the vocabulary of linguistics must be avoided.' Max Müller himself, who was one of the first to use the term 'Aryan race' (1861), abjured its biological interpretation and re-emphasized its purely linguistic significance. He wrote: 'To me an ethnologist who speaks of Aryan race, Aryan blood, Aryan eyes and hair, is as great a sinner as a linguist who speaks of a dolichocephalic dictionary or a brachycephalic grammar.' However, the concept of the 'Aryan race' had become so wide-spread that Müller's retraction and the views of Havet were without practical effect.

There is indeed a group or family of related languages labelled 'Indo-European' or 'Aryan'. Language, however, spreads and is transmitted from one people to another by migration, conquest and commercial exchanges, without, on that account, implying membership of the same biological human group by those speaking similar tongues.

The best illustration of this is to be found in the United States, whose 150 million citizens are a new type to which a multitude of races from all points of the world have contributed. Though the main strains of the population range from tall, long skulled blonds (Nordic type) through short, sub-brachycephalic blonds (Eastern European type) to tall, dark-skinned dolichocephalics (Atlantic-Mediterranean type), all of them speak English. In other words there are a number of groups somatically distinct with a common language, not to mention the numbers of English-speaking North American citizens of Negro, Amerindian, and Chinese stock.

In other words, a nation can consist of more than one race, while—conversely—biologically similar groups may be sub-divided into separate nations. The inhabitants of North America bear more resemblance to the people of Denmark and Sweden than to the people of south Germany, while the latter are physically akin to parts of the population of France, Czechoslovakia and Yugoslavia. How then is it possible to speak of German, Aryan or Anglo-Saxon 'races'?

Generalizations about the 'Aryan' race and its superiority are based on arguments which lack all objective validity and are erroneous, contradictory and unscientific.

It is in the strictly morphological field that the incongruities are greatest. Research into the skull formations and other characteristics of individuals or groups regarded as authentic 'Aryans', 'Teutons', 'Anglo-Saxons' and 'Celts' shows considerable variation alike in earlier ages and in our own. It is a proven fact that there have been both brachycephalics and dolichocephalics in Europe since the earliest ages. The work of von Holder, Lissauer, and Virchow (1870-80) demonstrated that the primitive population of the Baltic was morphologically heterogeneous with a large percentage of brachycephalics. In 1889 Virchow asserted: 'The typical Aryan postulated in theory has never been discovered' and even expressed the opinion that the brachycephalic was superior to the dolichocephalic. However, this was not enough to check belief in the superiority of the 'blond dolichocephalic', which had taken strong root in the popular imagination.

A moment came, however, when even the creators of the Aryan racial myth began to realize little by little that the physical types for which they claimed superiority and the 'inferior' non-Aryan were non-existent figments of the mind. Ammon himself admitted that he had never met a pure Alpine brachycephalic: 'Some brachycephalics were blond, others tall, others with narrow noses or with some other trait which they should not have had.'

However, the contradictions under this head reach their worst when Chamberlain, who had described the 'blond Teuton' type, concluded by denying all worth to anthropometry because it could give no indication of superiority. He admits that 'the Teutons of antiquity were not all dolichocephalic giants', but . . . 'a tentative examination of them would show us that all of them present the specific characteristics of the German people both physically and mentally'. He then asserts that this subjective appreciation 'teaches more than can be learnt in a congress of anthropology'. At one point he asks: 'In fact what type of man was the Aryan?' explains that philosophy, anthropology and ethnology cannot give an exact and detailed description of the Aryan people, and adds: 'Who knows what will be taught about the Aryans in 1950?'

He has no hesitation in asserting that 'the noble visage of Dante is indisputable proof of his Teutonic origin' (despite which Waltmann—as we have seen—thought Dante a product of miscegenation). Luther is also regarded as of Teutonic type although his traits are quite unlike Dante's (Luther was dolichocephalic while Dante was brachycephalic), but that does not prevent our author writing: 'Dante and Luther are at the two extremes of the noble range of physiognomy of the great men of the German race.' He concludes with another coruscating phrase: 'He who proves himself German by his deed is German, whatever his genealogy.'

In view of the physical heterogeneity of the supposed 'Nordic' or 'Aryan' (a good example of this would be an individual 'as tall as Goebbels, as blond as Hitler and as slim as Goering'), Nazism cast aside every pretence of biological justification for its imperialistic doctrine of the economic subjugation of other peoples and reached the conclusion that 'a Nordic soul may be joined to a non-Nordic body', and that 'the Nordic man may be recognized by his deeds and not by the length of his nose or the colour of his eyes' (*Nationalsozialistische-Korrespondenz,* June 1936).

The inference is clearly that in racism the physical criterion is a mere smokescreen, abandoned as useless when the circumstances of the moment require: 'The differentiation of the human races is not a matter of science; it is by immediate perception that we recognize emotionally the differences we call racial.' In the view of Dr. Gross (1934): 'Politics cannot wait until science has worked out a racial theory; politics must outstrip science with the intuitive basic truth of the diversity of blood between peoples and with its logical consequence, the principle of rule by the most gifted.'

Thus the origin of racism is not scientific but political. It is used by enemies to justify their fighting each other although they may be of similar racial composition, or by allies to discover a 'racial brotherhood' even when they are morphologically distinct. For instance Aryans should logically have regarded the Japanese people as inferior, a race of sub-men, on account of their colour. However, political pacts make compromise necessary, and the explanation was given that the white Ainus of Japan had interbred considerably with the yellow races and hence the Japanese today, while presenting the aspect of yellow men, 'nevertheless possess all the moral and intellectual qualities of an Aryan and even of a Nordic people'. On the strength of a theory so adaptable, Alfred Rosenberg (1935) was able to state officially that 'the Japanese leaders are as biologically reliable as the German'.

Ruth Benedict is in the right of it in saying: 'No distortion of anthropomorphic facts is too absurd to be used by propaganda backed by force and the concentration camp.'

CONCLUSION

The existence of individual somatic and psychic differences is a fact; in every race, nation, class or community, better and worse endowed individuals can be found. This is a biological fact to which there are no exceptions. The variations in question are however completely unconnected with the alleged superiority or inferiority of specific human groups.

That one's own family or race is better than any other is a belief of long standing. What is relatively new is the attempt to justify this alleged 'superiority' scientifically on the grounds of innate biological characteristics.

The growing discontent of the peoples of India, the development of racial feeling among the Negroes, and the self-confidence displayed by the Japanese, Chinese and Indonesian peoples, are among many proofs that the races hitherto despised for their supposed inferiority are every day less ready to accept the judgement on their qualities passed by certain elements in the white races.

Democracy recognizes the existence of differences between

men, but considers that *all men* possess the same inalienable rights and seeks to afford *all men* equal political, social and economic opportunities.

Totalitarianism also accepts the differences between men and peoples as inevitable but holds that they imply the principle of obedience to the will of a 'master' race expressed through 'superior men'. Its concern is to enslave all who are capable of falling-in with the will of the 'masters' and to exterminate all those unable to make themselves units in the totalitarian world.

As scientific discoveries and technological progress have largely destroyed the effectiveness of myth pure and simple among the masses, contemporary racism is accordingly forced to adopt a scientific disguise. Hence the racist myths of the twentieth century must seem to be based on science although, according to Prenant, it may be 'at the price of the most shameless falsifications and contradictions'. Racism has sought to capture and use for its own ends anthropology, the physiology of the blood, the laws of heredity, etc. But without success.

In 1918 the victorious allies rejected the proposal of the Japanese delegation to the Paris Conference of 1919 for the inclusion in the Charter of the League of Nations of a declaration proclaiming the equality of all races. Since 1945, however, the work of the United Nations Organization and its Specialized Agencies has been shared by tall blond dolichocephalics, short dark dolichocephalics, brachycephalics, yellow men, Negroes, halfbreeds and representatives of many nations differing in culture and morphology. All these varied elements drafted and unanimously approved in December 1948, the Universal Declaration of Human Rights, the second Article of which lays down that: 'Everyone is entitled to all the rights and freedoms set forth in the Declaration, without distinction of any kind, such as race, colour, sex, language, religion, political or other opinion, national or social origin, property, wealth or other status.'

The amazing assertion of Burgess (1890) in justification of German colonial policy—that the Germans 'are fully entitled to annex the territory of recalcitrants (the reference is to the native peoples) and transform it into the dwelling place of civilized man'—is a revealing instance of how the 'superiority' of the racist leads him to accept without concern for morality or law the criterion of power as the source of law where 'inferior' peoples are concerned.

47

There are two questions the answers to which will go far towards banishing racial myths. What degree of difference is possible between individuals of similar heredity living in unlike settings? And again, what are the differences between individuals differing in heredity and living in the same setting?

Differences between human beings should be regarded as facts requiring understanding and interpretation and not as qualities meriting blame or praise. Major Morton writes: 'Much of the friction between races, as between nations or individuals, is due to misunderstanding; if the peoples were willing to devote a little of their time to understanding each others' points of view they would often realize that things are not going as badly as they think' (1920).

Racial prejudice may spring from economic and political causes, from a particular race's superiority or inferiority complex, from biological differences, from hereditary instinct or from a combination of several of these causes. In every case matters are greatly aggravated by the tendency to accept theories and hypotheses without the slightest critical examination.

Doctrines of racial superiority have played an unprecedented role in the high policy of States. They have been the excuse for cruelty and inhumanity, they have served as a pretext for the colonial expansion of Europe and for modern imperialism, sharpened race hatred, carried patriotism to absurd lengths and promoted war.

Nothing will be achieved by promulgating new laws or enforcing compliance with the present laws, since the effectiveness of those laws is in direct proportion to the conviction of the majority of citizens of the need for them and their intrinsic rightness. More can be done against racial prejudices and myths by endeavouring to amend the conditions which give rise to them.

Fear is the first of these: fear of war, fear of economic insecurity, fear of loss of personal or group prestige, etc. Racial prejudice in one form or another will continue in the world as long as there is not a greater sense of personal security.

It is necessary to demonstrate the absurdity of regarding human groups en bloc as 'completely good' or 'completely bad'. Science, democratic beliefs and humanitarian feeling are at one in rejecting the condemnation of any man on the grounds of his race or colour or of his chancing to be in a state of slavery.

Racism is quite different from a mere acceptance or scientific and objective study of the fact of race and the fact of the present inequality of human groups. Racism involves the assertion that inequality is absolute and unconditional, i.e., that a race is inherently and by its very nature superior or inferior to others quite independently of the physical conditions of its habitat and of social factors.

The last half century has seen the development of a hypertrophied nationalism. The horrors of war and the anxieties of an armed peace are doing much to maintain it. The elimination, through individual and group conviction, of racial myths can exert a powerful influence and bring about a better spirit and better understanding in the relations between man and man.

BIBLIOGRAPHY

BENEDICT, Ruth. *Race, science and politics.* New York, 1941, 209 p.

BURNS, Alan. *Colour prejudice.* London, 1948, 171 p.

COMAS, Juan. *Existe una raza judía?* Mexico, 1941, 29 p.

—. *El mestizaje y su importancia social.* Mexico, 1944, 12 p.

—. *La discriminación racial en América.* Mexico, 1945, 27 p.

COUNTS, Earl W. *This is race.* An anthology selected from the international literature on the races of man. New York, 1950, 747 p.

DUNN, L. C. and DOBZHANSKY, Th. *Heredity, race and society.* New York, 1950, 165 p.

HANKINS, Frank H. *The racial basis of civilization: a critique of the nordic doctrine.* New York, 1926.

HUXLEY, Julian S. and HADDON, A. C. *We Europeans: a survey of 'racial' problems.* New York and London, 1936, 246 p.

KLUCKHOHN, Clyde. *Mirror for man.* New York, 1949, 313 p.

MONTAGU, M. F. Ashley. *Man's most dangerous myth. The fallacy of race.* New York, 1942, 304 p.

ORTIZ, Fernando. *El engaño de las razas.* La Havana, 1946, 428 p.

PARKES, James. *An enemy of the people, anti-semitism.* New York, 1946, 151 p.

PRENANT, Marcel. *Raza y racismo.* Mexico, 1939, 172 p.